Christmas Memories

MELODY BOBER

8 Early Intermediate to Intermediate Piano Arrangements of the Season's Most Nostalgic Carols

The Christmas season brings a flood of wonderful memories from my childhood: trips to my grandparent's farm where the 15-foot tree was ablaze with light; the continuous buffet of homemade holiday treats; and the fellowship of aunts, uncles and cousins. These things truly made the holiday one of love and happiness.

Christmas morning was always exciting with the opening of gifts and discovering the treasures from Santa in our stockings. The day was complete with the reading of the Christmas story from Luke, Chapter 2 and the singing of traditional Christmas carols.

In *Christmas Memories, Book 1,* I share arrangements of some of my favorite carols. It is my hope that you enjoy practicing and performing the arrangements in this collection and that they will stir your hearts and re-kindle your own precious memories of this blessed season.

Merry Christmas!

Melody Bober

Alfred

Copyright © MMVII by Alfred Publishing Co., Inc.
All Rights Reserved   Printed in USA

ISBN10: 0-7390-4914-3
ISBN13: 978-0-7390-4914-3

Jingle Bells

James Pierpont
Arr. by Melody Bober

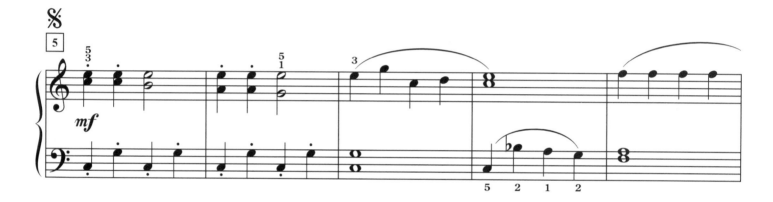

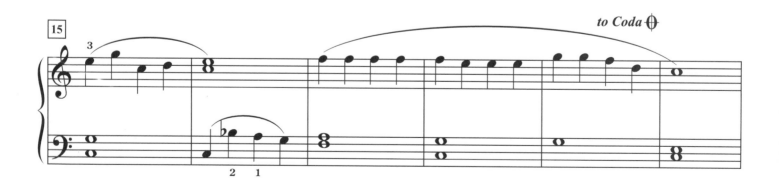

3

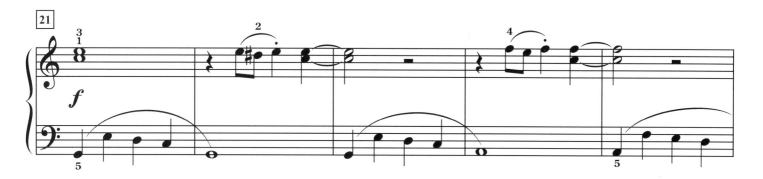

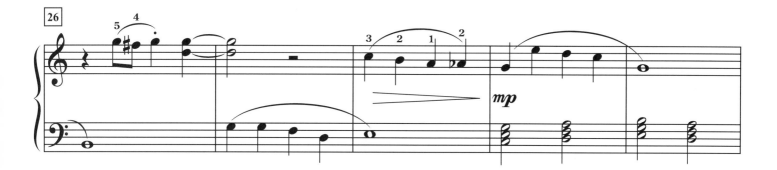

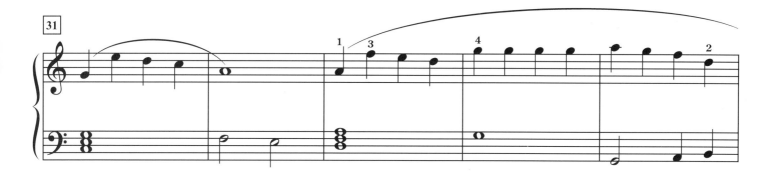

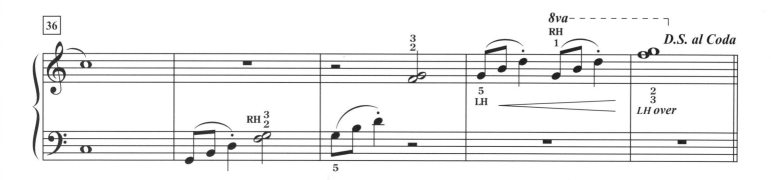

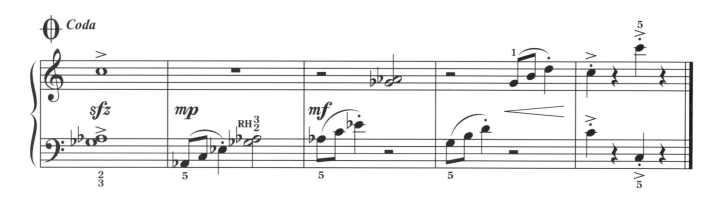

We Three Kings of Orient Are

John Henry Hopkins
Arr. by Melody Bober

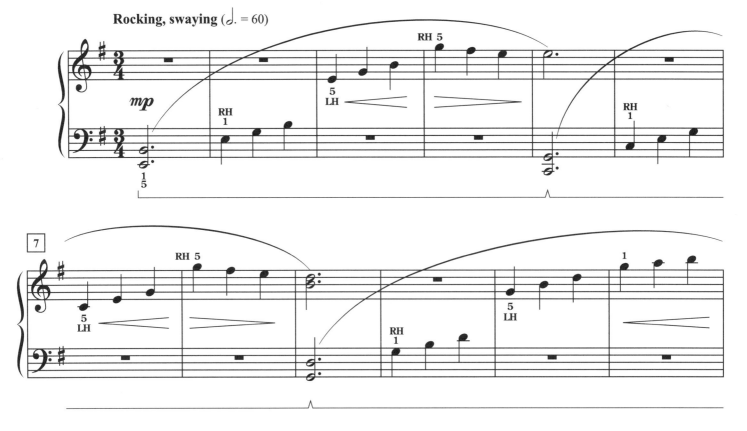

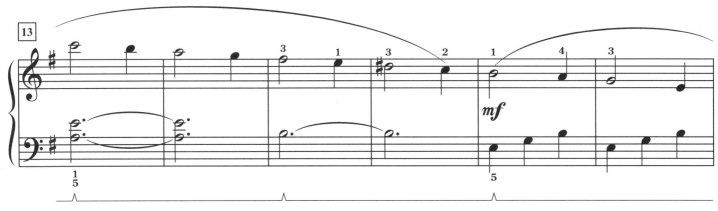

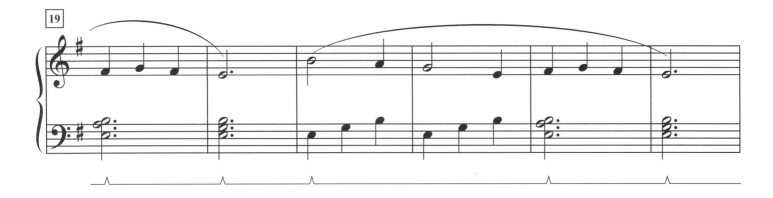

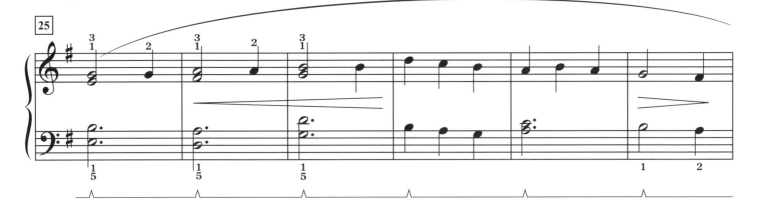

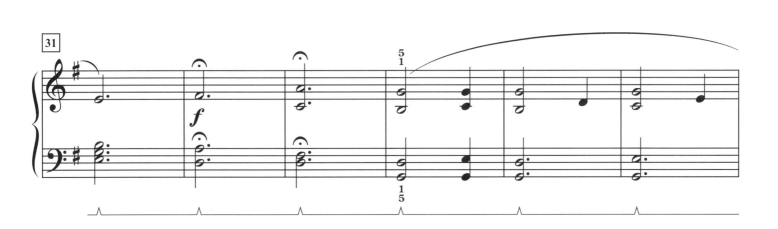

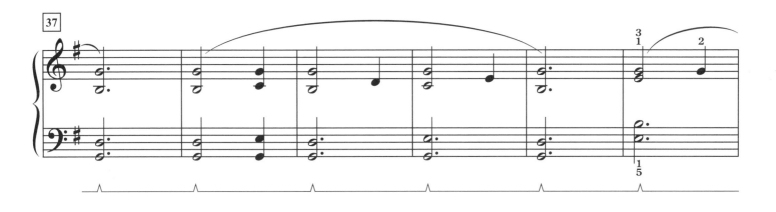

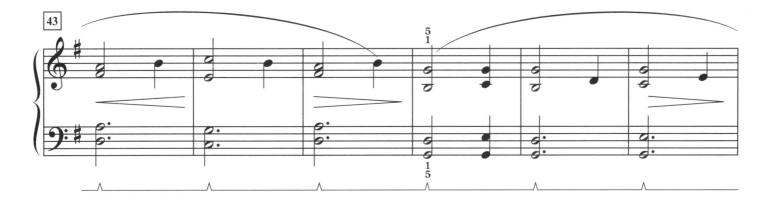

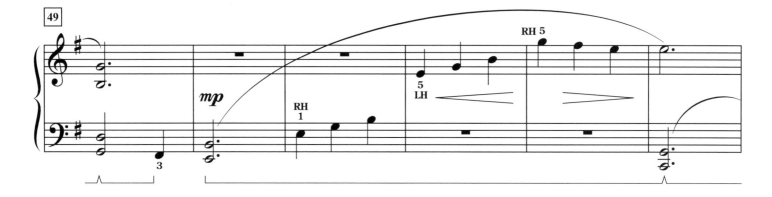

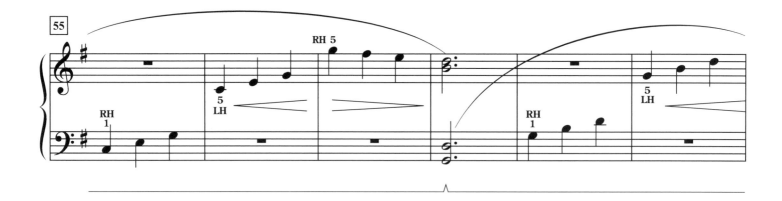

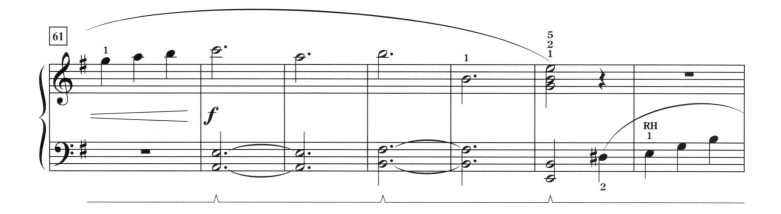

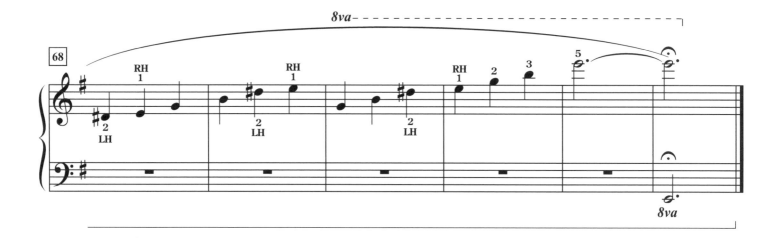

Deck the Halls

Welsh Carol
Arr. by Melody Bober

With spirit (♩ = 160)

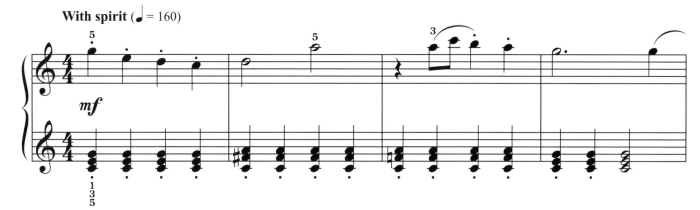

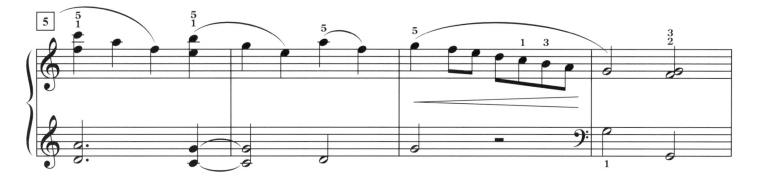

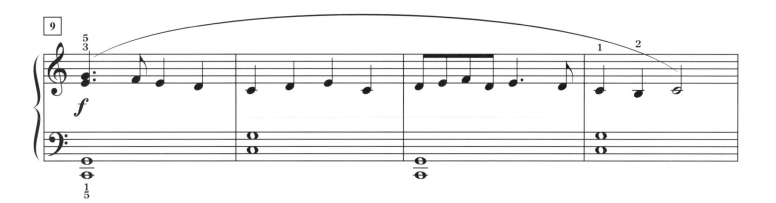

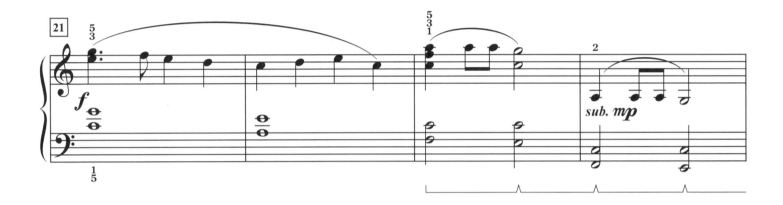

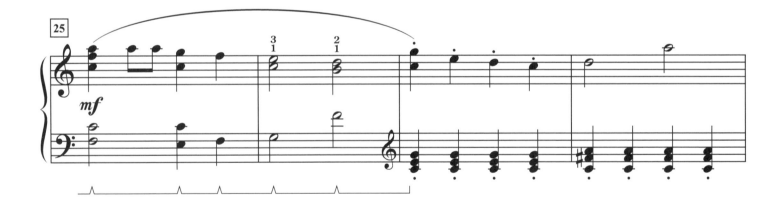

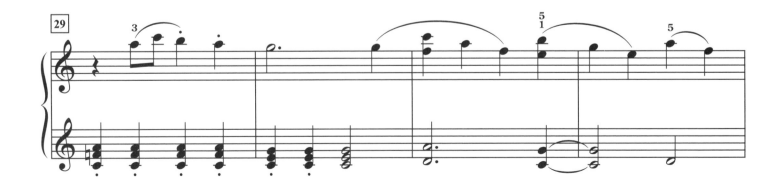

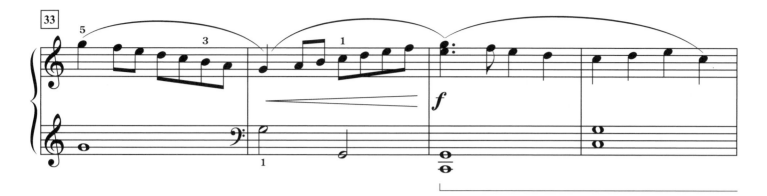

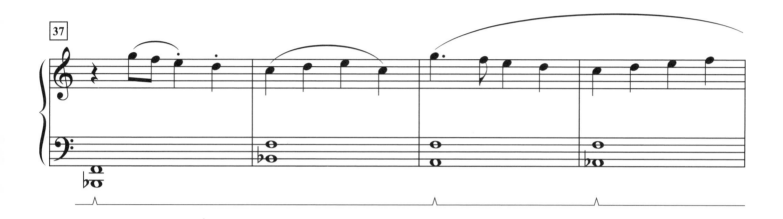

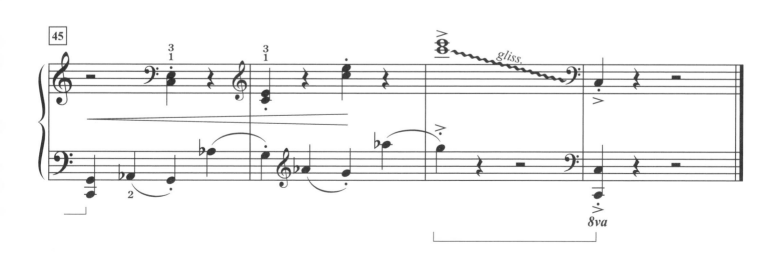

Carol of the Bells

Mykola Leontovich
Arr. by Melody Bober

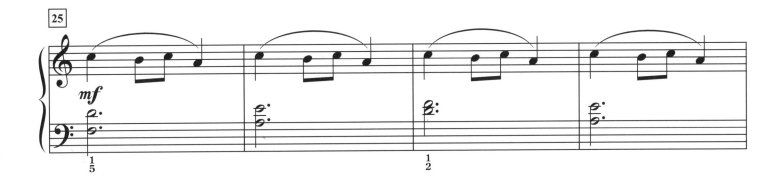

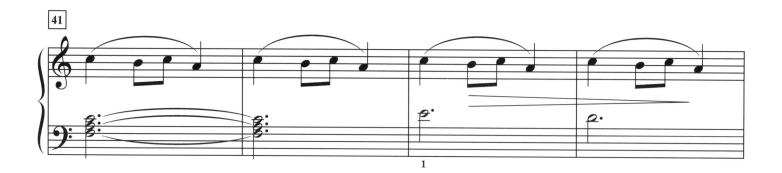

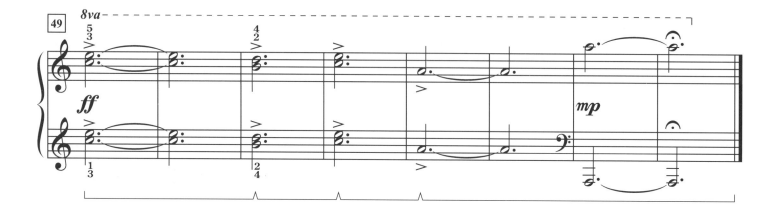

Up on the Housetop

B. R. Hanby
Arr. by Melody Bober

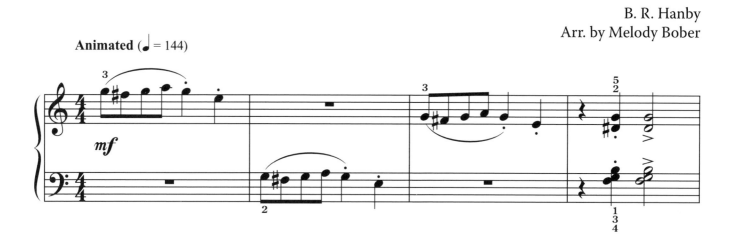

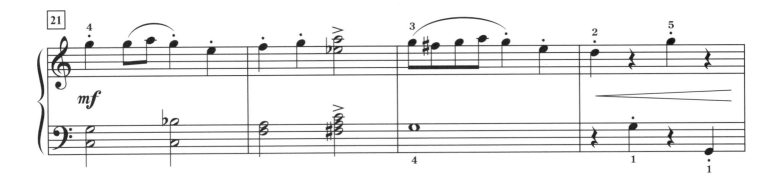

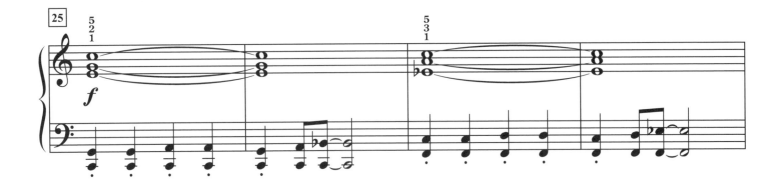

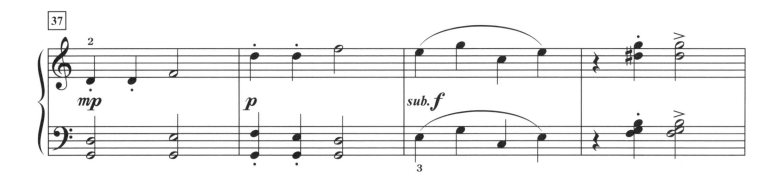

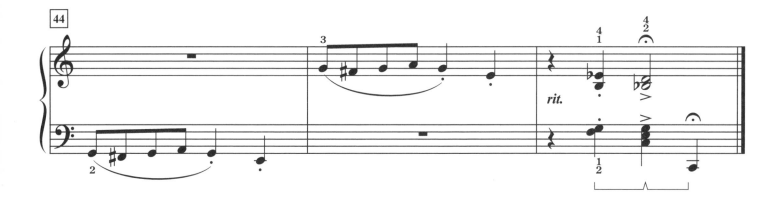

Silent Night

Franz Grüber
Arr. by Melody Bober

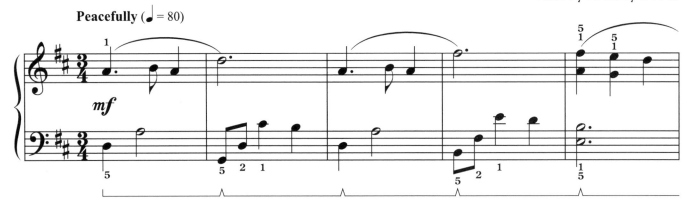

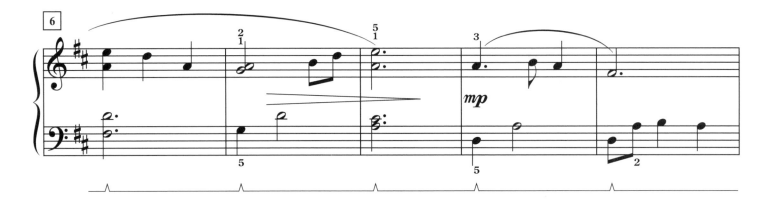

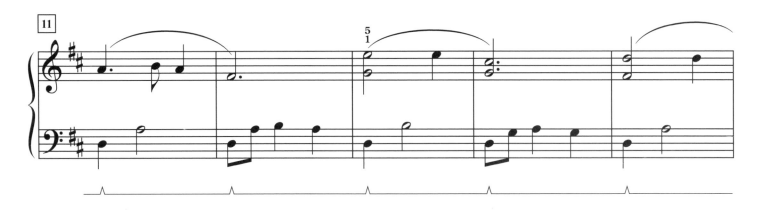

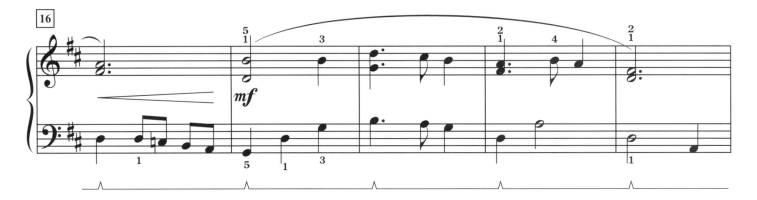

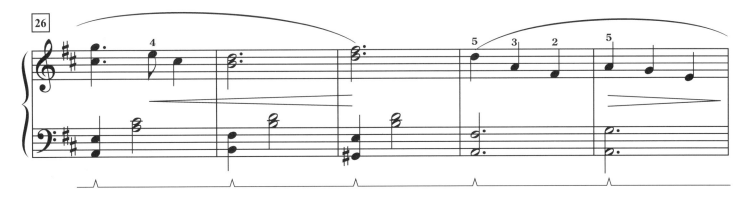

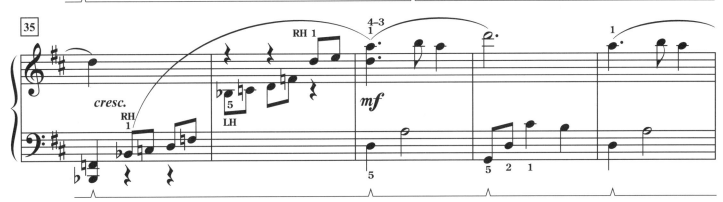

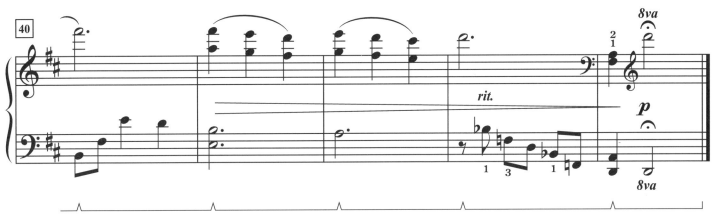

Theme and Variations on
We Wish You a Merry Christmas

Traditional
Arr. by Melody Bober

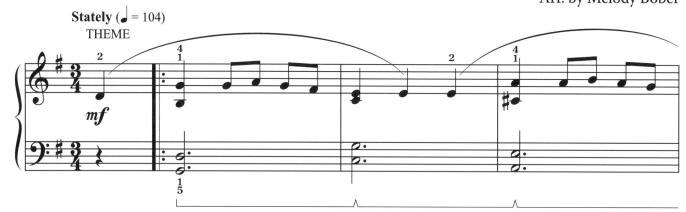

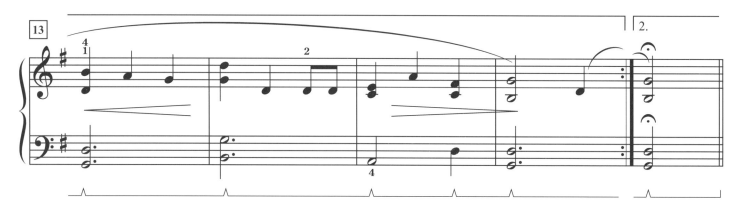

19

Boogie! (♩ = 126)
VARIATION 1

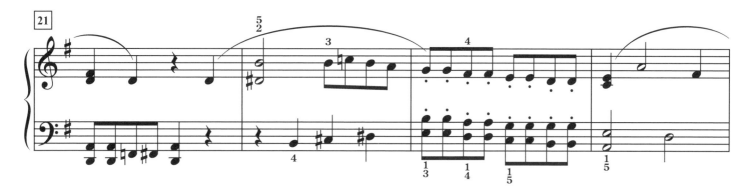

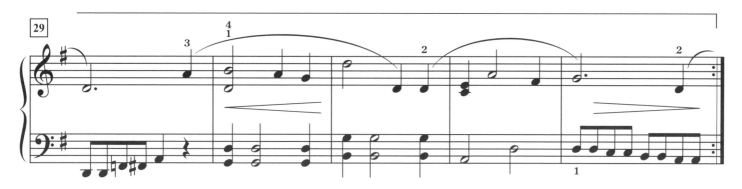

20

Classical waltz (♩ = 108–112)

VARIATION 2

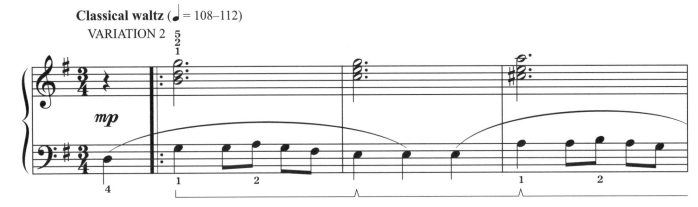

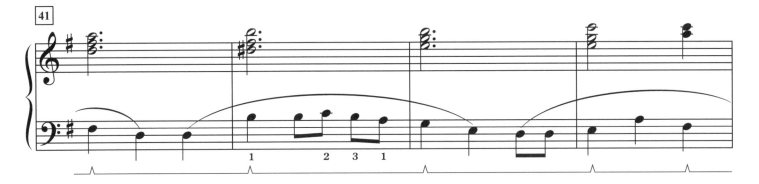

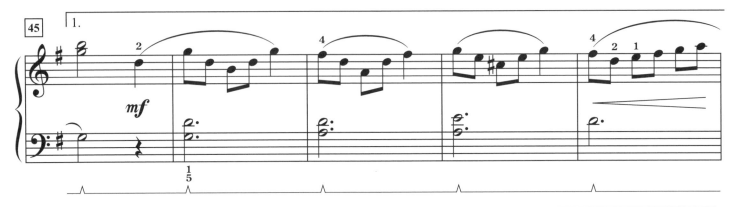

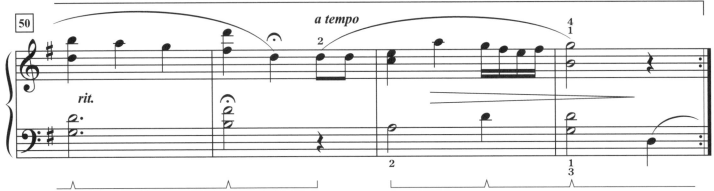

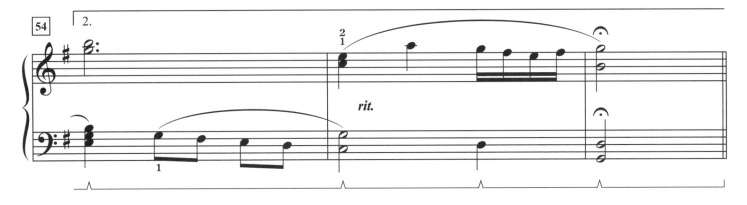

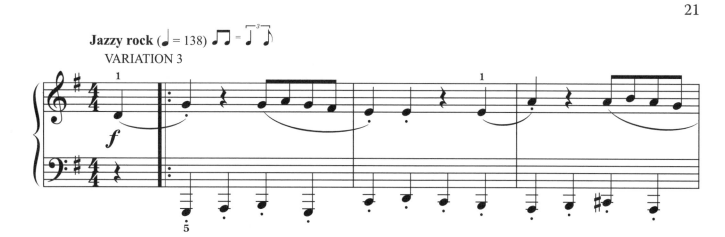

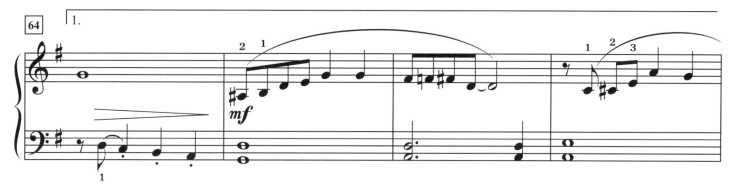

Angels from the Realms of Glory

Henry T. Smart
Arr. by Melody Bober

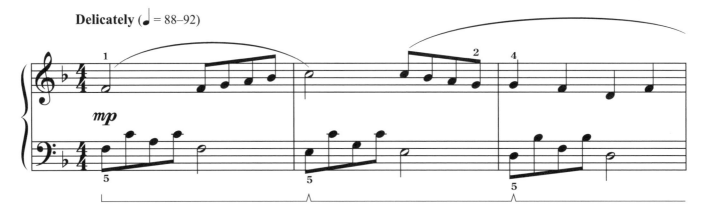

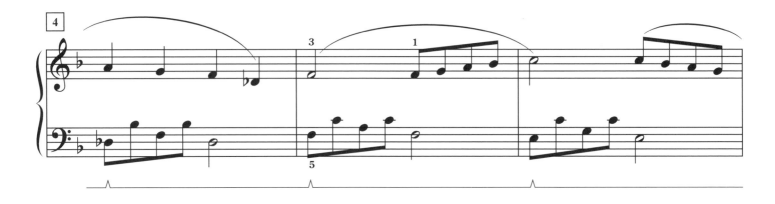

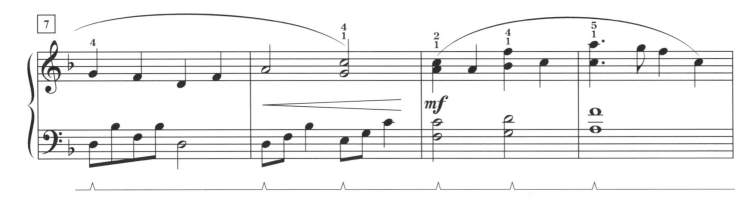

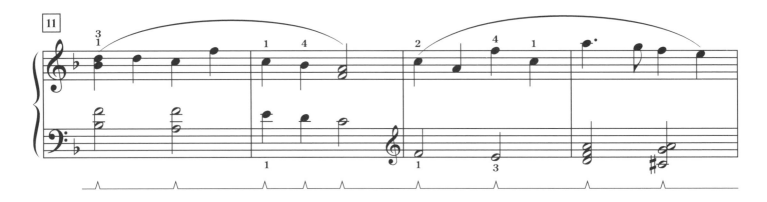

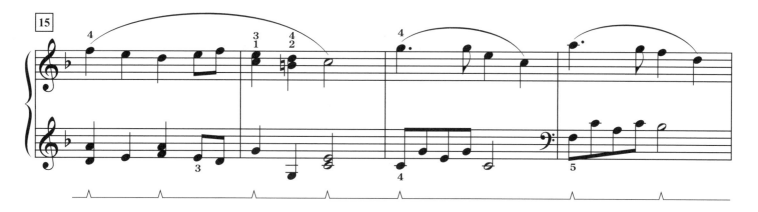

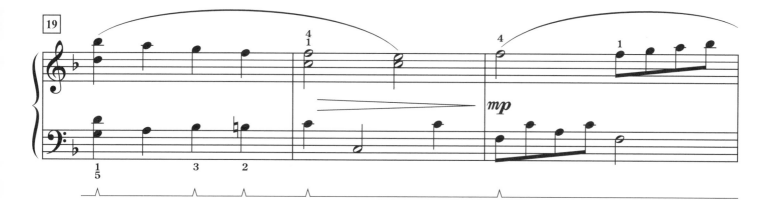

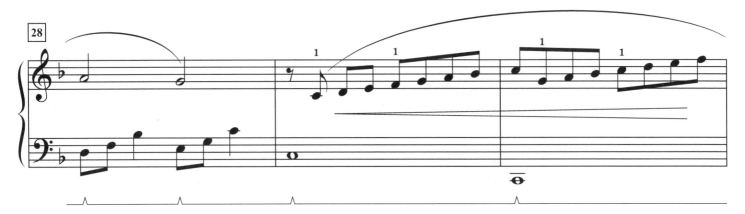

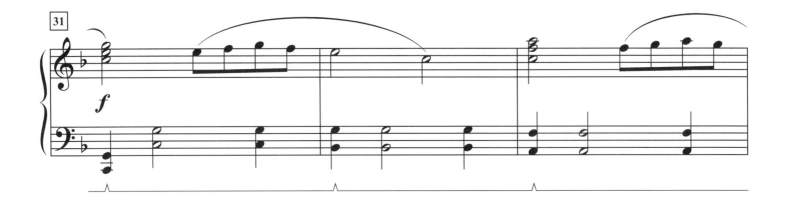